Original title:
The Lush Life

Copyright © 2025 Creative Arts Management OÜ
All rights reserved.

Author: Elias Marchant
ISBN HARDBACK: 978-1-80581-752-9
ISBN PAPERBACK: 978-1-80581-279-1
ISBN EBOOK: 978-1-80581-752-9

Savoring Eden

In a garden that's quite wild,
Squirrels dance, each tree a child.
Bees in suits, they buzz and hum,
Even snails join in the fun.

The tomatoes wear their finest red,
While pumpkins think they're quite the head.
Carrots giggle underground,
In this Eden, joy is found.

Nectar and Nectarines

Nectar drips from cheek to chin,
Juicy bites where dreams begin.
Fruit stands boasting their best picks,
Each peach plumper than a brick.

Baskets stacked and colors bright,
Taste buds dance in pure delight.
Sticky fingers, laughter reigns,
Nature's candy in our veins.

Citrus smiles on sunny days,
Tickling tongues in bright displays.
Giggling while we munch and chew,
Every slice a laughter's cue.

With lemonade in hand we toast,
For the fruit we love the most.
Savoring each juicy scene,
Life is sweet, and oh so keen!

Hushed Gardens at Dusk

Garden whispers come alive,
Evening's glow, the critters thrive.
Crickets serenade the breeze,
While fireflies do as they please.

Lavender sways, a gentle dance,
Insects buzz in twilight's trance.
Frogs in chorus, nightly song,
Harmonies where we belong.

With laughter echoed 'neath the stars,
Spilling secrets, near and far.
Tales of mischief, stolen sprigs,
Underneath the moon, we digs.

Petals sigh, the shadows blend,
Around the corner laughter wends.
Each garden's lull a funny tale,
In these hushed hours, we prevail.

Blooming Abundance

Flowers bursting, colors bright,
Pansies prancing, quite a sight.
Daisies gossip, oh, so loud,
While sunflowers stand tall and proud.

Violets drop their leafy guise,
Sharing secrets 'neath the skies.
In this riot of bloom and cheer,
Every petal whispers, 'Come near!'

Nature's Embrace

A willow waves with leafy arms,
Inviting critters with all its charms.
Grasshoppers leap in playful grace,
While frogs croak tunes of their own pace.

Clouds above play hide and seek,
While flowers giggle, cheek to cheek.
In this embrace of green and blue,
Nature laughs, and so should you.

The Sweet Aroma of Growth

Baking bread with blooms so sweet,
Honey drips from every treat.
Lavender whispers to the bees,
'Come, enjoy this fragrant breeze!'

Mint leaves dance with a zesty twirl,
While seeds begin to spin and swirl.
In gardens where the laughter flows,
Life's sweet aroma truly grows.

Whimsy Among the Vines

In a garden filled with glee,
I found a gnome sipping tea.
A squirrel danced on a vine,
While a cat claimed the sunshine.

Bees buzzed in goofy lines,
Wearing hats made of dandelions.
Each flower wore a silly grin,
Debating which one would win!

A World Touched in Green

Frogs in shades of neon green,
Playing leapfrog on the scene.
A parrot cracked a silly joke,
    As I tried not to choke!

Underneath the leafy crown,
I tripped on roots, fell down.
A raccoon offered me a chip,
Said, 'Join me for a snack trip!'

Foraging for Sunshine

Looking for light, I climbed a tree,
Where a squirrel tossed nuts at me.
The sun peeked through the leaves,
   To watch my clumsy retrieves.

I saw a worm with a top hat,
Strolling by on a crooked mat.
"Mind the puddle!" he did yell,
   As I landed with a splat!

Embrace of Abundant Life

A rabbit threw a wild party,
With snacks that were quite hearty.
Dancing with the buzzing flies,
And laughing at the clouds in the skies.

A salad spoke, "You can't eat me!"
While singing tunes from a nearby tree.
Life here is a comic spree,
Let's cheer for all the veggie glee!

Elysian Fields Come Alive

In fields where daisies dance and sway,
The cows are keen to join the play.
With butterflies that tell bad jokes,
And chickens poker-faced like blokes.

A picnic spread with pies galore,
The ants arrive, a tiny chore.
They steal the crumbs right from our hands,
While rabbits lead the conga bands.

Celebration in Every Leaf

A leaf fell down, it wore a hat,
It winked at squirrels, how about that?
The breeze sang tunes of joyful cheer,
While birds chirped puns that brought a sneer.

The flowers threw a vibrant bash,
With petals sharp as any clash.
They danced and twirled in colors bright,
While bees buzzed 'til the fall of night.

The Symphony of Growth

Roots below with stories deep,
A tree in thought, it starts to weep.
But don't be fooled by nature's prose,
For mushrooms giggle as it grows.

A cacophony of whining vines,
That tell tall tales of grape-filled wines.
With every sprout, a laughter loud,
The garden's like a ruckus crowd.

Emerald Canopy Serenade

Beneath the leaves of emerald sheen,
The critters hum a merry scene.
With branches swaying to a beat,
And squirrels putting on their feat.

The owls in tuxedos look so neat,
While raccoons bring some dance floor heat.
The moonlight casts a shimmering glow,
As nighttime critters steal the show.

The Allure of Summer

Sunshine slides on the lawn,
Ice cream drips and is gone.
Picnics filled with bright hues,
Sips of joy in all the blues.

Lemonade's a zesty show,
Bee in tow, stealing the glow.
Flip-flops dancing, what a scene,
Chasing shadows, feeling keen.

Watermelons smile wide,
Fruits and laughs they coincide.
Sunscreen splashes, sandy toes,
How the neighboring garden grows!

Chasing fireflies at night,
Twinkling, giving pure delight.
Summer's laughter fills the air,
Mirth is hiding everywhere.

Verdant Secrets Unraveled

Green leaves giggle with a twist,
Tickling secrets that can't be missed.
Every shadow holds a grin,
Nature's mischief tucked within.

Sunflowers strut in sunny hats,
While daisies gossip—who needs cats?
Winding paths of leafy cheer,
Every turn, a joke to hear.

Roots will laugh beneath the ground,
Spreading tales that bounce around.
Pollen's powder, a soft tease,
Tickles noses with such ease.

So let's wander, hand in hand,
Through this playful, vibrant land.
Verdant whispers filled with fun,
Nature's secrets, on the run!

Feasting on Nature's Gift

Berries bouncing on my plate,
A squirrel steals my lunch too late.
Mushrooms waltz with fairy glee,
I giggle at their jubilee.

Honey drips from trees up high,
While ants march in a neat line sly.
The picnic blanket flaps and flies,
As grasshoppers hop to my surprise.

Bright tomatoes blush with pride,
While cucumbers try to hide.
Nature serves a feast so bold,
Yet I can't bear the ants so cold!

With every crunch, I feel delight,
But squirrels plot by moonlit night.
So here's my toast to nature's cheer,
With a wink, I'll just steer clear!

Woods Whispering Abundance

In the woods, the trees all prance,
Branches sway, they love to dance.
A raccoon sings a silly tune,
While rabbits hop beneath the moon.

Leaves gossip under sun's warm rays,
Sharing secrets of their days.
"Who stole my acorns?" cries the jay,
His feathers ruffled, in dismay.

A chorus of frogs joins the show,
In a mud bath, they steal the glow.
The owls hoot with knowing flair,
As fireflies twinkle through the air.

So raise a mug to nature's zest,
In this wild world, I feel so blessed.
With laughter echoed through the trees,
Join in the fun, it's sure to please!

Silken Threads of Growth

In the garden, blooms wear crowns,
While worms wiggle in funny gowns.
Petals flutter like silly kites,
Tickled by breezes, oh what sights!

Sunflowers stretch their leafy arms,
While daisies display their little charms.
Bees buzz around in silly haste,
Dancing on nectar, a sweetened taste.

Vines entwine like friends in cheer,
As laughter fills the atmosphere.
A pumpkin's grin, oh what a sight,
As marigolds laugh through the night.

In this patch of joy so bright,
Growth is a dance, a pure delight.
So come and join the joyous show,
In nature's realm, let laughter flow!

Verdant Whispers

In a garden so bright, bees buzz and play,
Worms hold dance-offs as flowers sway.
The sun spills laughter on leaves so green,
While squirrels debate on whose turn to preen.

A tomato wore shades, feeling quite grand,
While cucumbers plotted in a secret band.
The salads conspire, it's all in good jest,
To be the favorite at the next lunchtime fest.

Sun-Kissed Reverie

Breakfast in bright light, toast takes a dip,
Butter melts into a full-on slip.
Juice oranges squeal as they hit the rim,
While pancakes take twirls on a syrupy whim.

A coffee mug winks from its chrome perch,
Sipping up gossip at the morning church.
The butter croissants giggle, puffed with cheer,
As muffins roll over, drinks all around here!

Tapestry of Greens

In the meadow, grass tickles my feet,
With daisies that laugh, feeling pretty neat.
And don't get me started on clovers so bold,
Holding tiny parties, their secrets untold.

The zucchini keeps jesting, 'I'm quite handsome!'
While radishes blush in their leafy land worth some.
They play charades as the kale strikes a pose,
Making greens famous with all their fine clothes.

Opulent Oasis

In a pool of cool bliss, ducks make a splash,
While lilies wave proudly, their petals all flash.
The fish crack up, spinning tales of the day,
As a frog in a hat hops along the way.

With pineapples gossiping under bright suns,
Coconuts chuckle, enjoying their runs.
In this paradise, brimming with cheer,
Every fruity friend feels like they're top-tier!

Vibrant Visions of Hidden Springs

In a place where the giggles bloom,
Fragrant scents fill every room.
Daisies dance, and bees do sway,
Each joke whispered lights the day.

Sipping nectar from a jar,
Dreams float in like a bright star.
A frog croaks the punchline loud,
Nature's laughter, joy unbowed.

Clouds scatter in playful jest,
As squirrels race, they never rest.
A splash! The fish leap in glee,
Oh, the fun of being free!

Sunlight winks from leafy greens,
Tickling toes in gentle streams.
A carnival of giddy sights,
Where giggles lead to wild delights.

Echoes of Fertile Heartstrings

Listen close to the whispering trees,
They chatter sweetly with the bees.
A monkey swings, a banana slips,
A chorus of laughter in joyful quips.

With each pluck of the heartstring's tune,
A raccoon waltzes 'neath the moon.
He trips on roots, but grins all the same,
In this garden, laughter's the game.

Faces bright, a vibrant cast,
Winter's chill forgotten fast.
With jokes baked in every pie,
A feast of chuckles under the sky.

In the shadows where humor thrives,
Every creature, hilariously alive.
So hold your sides and laugh anew,
This bounty's rich, and merry too!

Chasing Sun-drenched Shadows

Running wild in fields of gold,
Chasing stories yet untold.
Frolicking in patches of light,
Every moment feels just right.

A juggler spins his wobbly act,
While frogs leap with their own impact.
Giggles ripple through the air,
Sun-drenched shadows without a care.

With kites soaring high above,
Each tug a lesson in sweet love.
A tumble here, a playful shout,
In this game, there's never doubt.

From the sun, we catch our wishes,
Like fish that leap for joyful dishes.
In every giggle, there's a chase,
Life's funny dance, a warm embrace.

Banquet Under the Leaves

A feast laid out on green delight,
With dandelion cups, oh what a sight!
Squirrels serve up acorns with cheer,
While all around, the laughter's near.

A bear brings pies, a sight to see,
Clumsy paws, but spirits free.
Berries burst in happy bites,
Moments shared in joyful sights.

As ants parade in fancy hats,
With a wink, they dance and chat.
Slippery spills cause raucous fun,
Each bite's a tale under the sun.

Echoes of laughter fill the glade,
In this banquet that nature made.
A toast to joys, a hearty cheer,
Under leafy roofs we gather near!

Citrus Dreams and Stardust

In a garden where lemons play,
Limes dance and twirl all day,
With oranges laughing in the sun,
Juicy jokes are quite the fun.

Lemonade rivers flow with cheer,
Grapefruit giggles are crystal clear,
Citrus pals in a wacky race,
Zesty smiles light up the place.

Flourishes of the Soul

In a world of wild, green pranks,
Frogs in bow ties join the ranks,
Dancing daisies with flair so bold,
Tickle your fancy, or so I'm told.

Birds wearing hats sing silly songs,
As squirrels declare they can't do wrongs,
Nature's jesters, a quirky whole,
Bringing laughter to every soul.

Flavors of the Overgrown

In the jungle where pineapples smile,
Coconuts giggle; come stay a while,
Bananas slip on jokes, oh dear,
Peeling away the mundane fear.

Jungle vines do salsa with flair,
Mangoes whisper secrets in air,
Overgrown flavors, a fruity spree,
Join the party, it's wild and free!

The Richness of Every Shade

Colors bursting like candy stores,
Purple berries, and bright green chores,
Pastel petals tumble in glee,
Nature's palette, a sight to see.

With each hue comes a quirky tale,
Gallivanting grasshoppers set sail,
In the richness of vibrant delight,
Life's a canvas, all colors unite!

Overgrown Rhythms

In the garden where laughter grows,
Flowers dance as the wind blows.
Bees buzzed in their silly race,
Sipping sweet nectar with a grin on their face.

Chickens cluck in a comical line,
Counting each worm, oh how divine!
While rabbits hop in a prancing jig,
Playing hide and seek, it's quite a gig.

The sun peeks through, a playful tease,
While tomatoes gossip with the bees.
Pumpkins chuckle in their round, bright cheer,
In this riot of colors, no room for fear.

So join the fun, let your worries go,
In this wild garden, let the good times flow.
For nature's stage is a quirky spree,
Where every riot of growth sings out with glee.

Delights in Blooming Abundance

Petals sing in the warm sunlight,
Tickling the leaves, oh what a sight!
Berries giggle, plump and round,
While butterflies pirouette all around.

Grasshoppers leap with a comedic flair,
Joking about who's the fairest of hair.
Mice exchange tales of cheese and bread,
In this festive field, nothing's left unsaid.

The fruit trees flaunt their juicy wear,
Dropping sweet treasures here and there.
Each bite's a joke, oh, what a tease,
Laughter ripples through the breeze.

Join this circus of thrill and fun,
Where nature's punchline cannot be outdone.
In the garden's embrace, let joy reign bright,
As we dance with delight until fall of night.

Harmony of Abundant Whispers

Whispers float through the leafy maze,
Squirrels chattering in comical ways.
Birds telling stories with a feathery flair,
Each note a laugh in the floral air.

Here, sunflowers wear their hats so tall,
Waving like friends at a carnival.
Cranberries chuckle in their fruity clumps,
While bunnies bounce and perform little jumps.

Oh, how the vegetables gossip at noon,
Murmuring secrets of the dancing moon.
Every sprout has a tale to unfold,
In this patch of humor, let the joy be told.

So sway with the rhythm, let your heart sway,
In this comedy show, come join the play.
For even the weeds wear a smile today,
In the harmony of laughter, come what may.

Succulent Serenade Under Stars

The night blooms with a starry cheer,
Cacti crack jokes about the moon's rear.
Succulents stretch in a sultry pose,
Sipping dew drops, speaking in prose.

Crickets play their symphonic release,
While frogs ribbit in a chorus of peace.
Twirling owls in their whimsical flight,
Creating mischief beneath the soft light.

Lavender sighs in a fragrant hum,
Tickling the noses of creatures dumb.
Each petal winks as the night wears on,
Making mischief from dusk until dawn.

So gather 'round for a midnight spree,
Join the plants in their jolly jubilee.
In this succulent world, let laughter erupt,
As nature's serenade leads us unstuck.

Elysium in Every Petal

In gardens where the bees just hum,
A butterfly lands with a little thrum.
Daisies dance in sunlight's kiss,
While ants march on, they can't resist.

The tulips gossip, so bright and bold,
About the roses, their stories told.
Each petal flutters, a tale to share,
Of sunlit moments and fragrant air.

Lilies laugh at the pond's reflection,
While frogs leap in, causing quite the commotion.
With every hop, a splash and a cheer,
Nature's jesters, loud and clear.

In this realm of color and glee,
A lounge for critters—come join, you'll see.
With every step, a giggle grows,
Elysium hides in the petals' prose.

Nature's Luxuriant Giving

A squirrel with flair, in a nutty disguise,
Swings from branches, under bright skies.
He hoards not gold, but acorns for fun,
Laughing at life, in the warmth of the sun.

Marigolds chuckle, a radiant glow,
Tickling each bumblebee racing below.
"They buzz like mad, those furry delight,
Pollinating dreams, in the glowing light!"

The trees share whispers, a cheeky breeze,
Waving their leaves, with such playful ease.
Each gust of wind calls forth a jest,
Nature's smirk at its very best.

In this realm where fun does abound,
Hearts grow lighter, joy can be found.
Join the frolic, don't be aloof,
Here's a cupcake for every goof!

Banquet of Breath and Bloom

At dawn's first blush, a feast unfolds,
With flowers dressed in hues of gold.
Petals plump up, ready to dine,
On droplets of dew, how divine!

The daisies chatter, "What's on the plate?"
"Some sunshine, a dash of love, just wait!"
While daffodils hop in a conga line,
Sharing sweet secrets, feeling just fine.

"Pass the pollen," cried the busy bee,
"It's just like sugar, sweet as can be!"
With laughter and color, they dance and sway,
In this banquet where joy steals the day.

So bring your smiles, join the delight,
Nature's party—everything feels right.
With every breath, let happiness loom,
At this quirky banquet, when flowers bloom!

Verdant Daydreams

In fields of green, the grass holds court,
Mice in bow ties, planning a sport.
With acorn caps like hats of fun,
They play all day 'til the setting sun.

The clouds float by on popcorn fluff,
While worms debate if they're quite tough.
"Let's stretch and wiggle," says one little friend,
"Life's a good joke, our twist never ends!"

Caterpillars strut in their flashy attire,
Practicing moves for their dance with desire.
As butterflies watch, sipping on dew,
They laugh at the antics of squirrels and crew.

In this realm of whimsy, so light on the soul,
Life's a grand game, an endless stroll.
With each verdant dream, embrace the scene,
Nature's humor shines bright and keen!

Opulence in Bloom

In a garden where the roses play,
Fluffy clouds dance, hip-hip-hooray!
Goldfish wear sunglasses, oh what a sight,
Chairs first-class, they take flight!

Twirling peacocks strut with flair,
Champagne fountains spraying everywhere.
A cat in a tux is the mayor here,
Laughing so hard, you'll shed a tear!

Daisies giggle at the sun's bright glow,
While juicy fruits form a row, row, row.
Sunbathers in hats made of cheese,
Sipping nectar with utmost ease!

But watch out for the grapes on the chase,
They roll wildly, a slippery race.
In this garden, life's a fancy jest,
Where merriment thrives, and humor's blessed.

Silk and Honey Dappled Days

Butterflies wear capes, ready to twirl,
While bees hold a party, all things swirl.
Pineapples in pajamas strut about,
Sipping sweet nectar, there's no doubt!

Marzipan clouds float by in pairs,
Where laughter and joy fill the air.
Berries gossip, spilling some tea,
Under glittery branches of a cherry tree!

Cushions of silk beneath a sunbeam,
Dancing with shadows, what a dream!
Ice cream cones with legs on the run,
Chasing rainbows, oh, isn't it fun?

Who wants a nap when life's a play?
Come and stretch in this grand day!
With giggles undying, all fuss fades away,
In a world where humor is here to stay!

The Garden of Excess

In a plot where jellybeans grow from the ground,
Chocolates swing on branches, all around.
Ducks wear tiaras, having a ball,
While juggling their eggs, they never fall!

Cakes in tuxedos, so classy and sweet,
Skipping about on tiny, swift feet.
Frogs on lily pads sing classic tunes,
While milking the sun, wearing full moons!

Rainbow fountains splash joy in the crowds,
As curly fries dance, twirling like clouds.
Hamburger castles stand tall and grand,
With ketchup rivers, a sauce-filled land!

But don't eat too much, or you'll float away,
On a marshmallow cloud, what a crazy stay!
In this garden of dreams, oh, what a guess,
Where laughter blooms like a flower, no less!

Vibrant Echoes of Paradise

Rainbows giggle as they weave through the air,
While turtles dance with a dash of flair.
Fruit bats wearing hats, flying in style,
Join the conga line, let's dance for a while!

Velvet beans sprout jazz hands with glee,
While frosty melons roll down to the sea.
Every step echoes with a cheerful beat,
In this paradise, life's a stony feat!

So come on, join the fiesta parade,
Where the joy is never delayed.
Lemons in tuxedos serve up the cheer,
While the guacamole winks, "Come over here!"

In vibrant colors, let laughter ignite,
As the silly echoes carry through the night.
Step in this rhythm, loose and free,
Where paradise sings — oh, what glee!

Lavish Chords of Earth

In gardens where the flowers sigh,
The bees hop by, they make me cry.
They dance around like they own the place,
With pollen stuck all over their face.

The veggies sing in colors bright,
Carrots boast of their orange light.
Potatoes lurk, looking quite shy,
Yet still they sport a tasty tie.

The sunbeams wink from skies so blue,
While lazy clouds swirl just for a view.
This joyful scene's a silly show,
Where even weeds put on a glow.

Resplendent Raindrops' Dance

Raindrops twirl on silver beams,
They dress the world in soft dreams.
Puddles pop like party balloons,
As splashes leap to jazzy tunes.

The frogs applaud with froggy glee,
They croak their joy, oh what a spree!
The ducks parade, a feathery band,
While worms take cover, quite unplanned.

Umbrellas twirl like dancers bold,
As weather forecasts break the mold.
In puddle rivers, kids roam free,
With rubber boots, it's jubilee!

Bucolic Bliss in the Twilight

The sun dips low, the shadows grow,
While fireflies start their evening show.
They flicker 'round with cheeky flair,
A tiny lanterns that dance in air.

The crickets chant their nightly tune,
While owls hoot out a wise cartoon.
With grass stains high, the children play,
In twilight's glow, they laugh away.

The stars poke through, with winks and grins,
As sleepy towns curl up like twins.
In cozy homes, the laughter weaves,
A fabric soft as autumn leaves.

The Tapestry of Opulent Green

In lush domains where colors collide,
The ferns stand tall, they take great pride.
The squirrels giggle, with acorns galore,
While chipmunks scheme by the forest door.

With every step, the earth ticks loud,
As nature twirls beneath a cloud.
The hedgehogs roll, they hold a ball,
While bees parade, they're having a ball.

Beneath a tree, friends gather near,
Where stories bloom, and laughter's clear.
In the tapestry of this delight,
Every day's a vivid sight.

Graze of Glorious Colors

In gardens where the daisies play,
The butterflies have lost their way.
They sip the nectar, oh so sweet,
While ants throw parties at our feet.

A rainbow spilled across the ground,
With candy-colored blooms abound.
The sun makes all the petals dance,
While bees compete for a sweet romance.

Each fruit is like a jester's grin,
Laughing as it rolls on in.
A watermelon wearing shades,
At picnics where the laughter fades.

So grab a plate and take a seat,
Join in the feast, the fruits so neat.
In this delightful, funny spree,
Life's glorious colors shout with glee!

The Art of Bountiful Living

In kitchens where the spices bloom,
And garlic dances with a broom.
A pinch of salt and lots of cheer,
The dinner table's drawing near.

A chef in a hat that's far too big,
Whisking eggs with quite the jig.
Flour clouds like buttered dreams,
As laughter fills the kitchen seams.

The fridge is bursting at the seams,
With leftovers that have lost their dreams.
Each jar a tale of culinary fun,
In this wild art, we all have won!

So raise a toast to every dish,
Fulfillment found, a belly's wish.
In kitchens bold and flavors bright,
The funny art of living light!

Nectar's Sweet Embrace

With honey dripped from golden spouts,
And fruits that tease with squeaky shouts,
A nectar river flows with glee,
As squirrels plan a fruit-filled spree.

The bees collaborate on their dance,
In floral skirts, they twirl and prance.
A juicy peach whispers, 'Take a bite,'
While citrus fruits are feeling bright.

When strawberries wear their best red capes,
They giggle at the pickers' scrapes.
A lemonade stand made of dreams,
Where laughter fills all the sunbeams.

So savor life's sweet, sticky song,
Where all the fruits and folks belong.
In this embrace, so rich and grand,
We find the laughter, hand in hand!

Crescendo of Flourishing Life

In meadows where the wee ones run,
Chasing shadows just for fun.
The daisies hold a talent show,
While clouds above are putting on a glow.

The sun shimmies in a golden dress,
As laughing squirrels make a mess.
Each leaf has stories, whispers loud,
About the antics of the crowd.

The rivers sing a bubbling tune,
As frogs indulge in their cartoon.
With every splash, the laughter grows,
In concert with the wind that blows.

So join this lively, funny chase,
In nature's grand and vibrant space.
With every chuckle, every cheer,
Life flourishes, oh so dear!

Vibrant Tales from the Thicket

In the thicket, laughter swells,
Where squirrels dance, and mischief dwells.
A frog in a top hat sings out loud,
While snappy crickets gather a crowd.

Frogs debate the best flies to eat,
As ants parade on tiny feet.
The trees lean in to hear the jive,
In this wild world, it's fun to thrive.

Bumblebees wear shades, looking cool,
While daisies gossip, breaking the rule.
A squirrel's acorn hits a friend,
And amidst the laughter, joys extend.

Oh, what a tale of antics bold,
In the thicket's heart, treasures unfold.
With every chuckle and silly sight,
Life's merry dance is pure delight.

Remnants of the Gracious Grove

In the grove, where giggles roam,
A raccoon finds an old ice cream cone.
He wears it proudly, like a crown,
While owls watch closely, never a frown.

Under branches, stories weave,
Silly shadows, make you believe.
A deer in socks prances by,
With a wink and a hop, oh my!

Beneath the leaves, a party's begun,
With caterpillars, it's all in fun.
They dance the night away with glee,
While fireflies hum a merry spree.

Oh, to be in this vibrant realm,
Where laughter is king, none can overwhelm.
In this grove, the breezes play,
With echoes of joy, come what may.

Tides of Green Emotions

The waves of green, they ebb and flow,
With giggling petals in a row.
A turtle riding waves of grass,
Chasing butterflies as they pass.

A fish once dreamed of landlike spree,
Now hops about, with endless glee.
A sardine in a bowl of pranks,
Makes splashy waves in silly ranks.

Grassy hills wear happy faces,
As rabbits race through all the bases.
The world's a stage of vibrant hues,
A comedy brewed in nature's views.

Oh, swirling joy from turf to sea,
In this realm, we dance so free.
With laughter's compass, hearts in flight,
The tides of fun shine ever bright.

Spice and Shade in Bloom

In the garden, where spices sing,
Sunshine whispers, joy's the thing.
A tomato's joke leaves peppers red,
While lilies giggle at what's said.

Amidst the shade, a secret fair,
With mushrooms swaying without a care.
A raccoon in sunglasses takes a seat,
In this quirky world, fun's a treat.

The chives crack puns, oh what a thrill,
While daffodils puff up with chill.
A beetroot's blush tells tales untold,
In the bloom of spice, life's bright and bold.

Oh, how laughter shades the scene,
In this garden, all's evergreen.
With each petal's giggle, we embrace,
The rich, the wild, in nature's grace.

Potpourri of Natural Wonder

In gardens green, a curious shoe,
Where daisies dream of a dance or two.
A ladybug snickers, tickling a leaf,
While squirrels debate their next nutty belief.

Sunbeams bounce like kids on a spree,
A chubby bumblebee sings off-key.
The daisies giggle, a riot in bloom,
As butterflies order up sunshine and gloom.

Resplendent Offerings in Earth's Embrace

Fruits hang ripe, a colorful bunch,
Banana peels cause an accidental punch.
Melons grinning with silly faces,
Pumpkins wish they could win races.

Roots twist and twirl in the earthy bed,
While radishes gossip on what was said.
Dirt-styled hair and smudged up shoes,
Nature's party, there's nothing to lose.

Livelihood in Every Sway

Grassy meadows play hide and seek,
A winded willow whispers, 'Something unique!'
The frogs croak jokes, ribbiting away,
While crickets dance in the spotlight's sway.

Clouds are puffs of cotton candy dreams,
As rainbows giggle in sunlight beams.
A squirrel in spectacles recites a note,
Claiming poetry isn't just for the goat!

Unveiling Layers of Bliss

Peppers prance in a colorful clan,
Eggplants wear hats like a fancy man.
Tomatoes blush when the sun says 'hello',
While zucchini spins in a veggie show.

A pickle floats in a briny pond,
Pasta noodles dream of a midnight fond.
Carrots debate if they're orange or green,
Life in the garden is laid back, serene.

Abundant Breaths of Nature

In gardens bright with colors wide,
The bees in bowler hats collide.
With flowers dancing, quite a show,
They buzz along in rows, you know.

The trees wear crowns, a leafy spree,
While critters plot with glee and glee.
The squirrels play tag, a furry race,
As sunlight spills with cheeky grace.

The flowers droop at cocktail hour,
With roses sipping from a flower-power.
A daisy hopes to win a prize,
But tulips know all the best lies.

As nature laughs and swings about,
The frogs start crooning, loudly shout.
Just breathe it in, this splendid play,
In every bloom, a joke on display.

Petals and Prowess

In fields where petunias throw a fit,
The daisies prance, not caring a bit.
With wiggly worms as their dance crew,
A flora twist, they shake right on cue.

The tulips flaunt their bright attire,
While bumblebees aspire higher.
A thistle tries to join the fun,
But prickles keep him on the run.

Sunflowers flex in golden hue,
With big smiles, they wink at you.
All petals proud, they twirl and reel,
In petal pageants, it's quite the deal!

As nature struts with zany flair,
A butterfly slips, what a scare!
With laughter echoing through the breeze,
Let's toast to nature's quirks with ease.

Bounty Beneath the Sun

The fruits hang low, a vibrant show,
Bananas wear hats like a carnival glow.
While giggling grapes play peek-a-boo,
The cherries throw a fruity crew.

Tomatoes blush, oh what a sight!
A cabbage roars with leafy might.
With carrots dancing in the shade,
Each root a star, a masquerade!

The corn keeps popping, what a blast,
While pumpkin dreams float by so fast.
They joke and jive, a merry bunch,
With every crunch, they share a punch.

As radishes tumble with great delight,
And lemons giggle in pure sunlight.
This bounty bursts, it's purest fun,
A harvest party! Let's not shun.

Glistening Threads of Nature's Tapestry

The spider weaves with utmost flair,
A gossamer net catching air.
With dew as diamonds all aglow,
Her artistry takes center show.

The flowers sway, a colorful quilt,
In morning's light, with magic built.
Beetles strut in tiny boots,
While butterflies gossip about their roots.

The sun dips low, a painter's brush,
While crickets start a twilight hush.
Each leaf a note in nature's score,
As laughter echoes, hear it roar.

In threads of green and blooms that sing,
A tapestry of joy takes wing.
With every stitch, a tale we weave,
In nature's arms, we laugh and believe.

A Flourish of Life

In a garden filled with cheer,
Squirrels dance, drink a beer.
Flowers wear their bright sun hats,
And giggling frogs share laughs with cats.

Bumblebees in tiny cars,
Zoom around like shooting stars.
Petunias whisper juicy tales,
While daisies flaunt their dainty trails.

The sun shines down, a playful prank,
As raindrops join in, making a clank.
Butterflies bow in vibrant skirts,
While worms in suits do antics that flirt.

Nature's stage, a grand delight,
Where every creature takes to flight.
In this flourish, laughter grows,
And joy sprouts up where the wind blows.

Playground of Flora

In the meadow, kids run wild,
Chasing dreams like a playful child.
Grasshoppers leap with tiny glee,
While daisies sway in harmony.

The sunbeam slides down the slide,
With rays of gold that simply glide.
Ladybugs hold races on the ground,
As giggles grow, laughter unbound.

Tulips spin like merry-go-rounds,
While cheeky gnomes tell funny sounds.
The roses blush at silly jokes,
And even pine trees crack their oaks.

In this playground, life's a game,
Each bloom and bug can stake a claim.
With petals bright and joy that flows,
It's a carnival where laughter grows.

The Empress of Green

In the kingdom of emerald might,
A sassy fern throws all her light.
She wears a crown of ivy leaves,
And reigns where sunshine always weaves.

Her subjects dance, oh what a sight,
The poppies twirl, sparks of delight.
With dandelions as her jesters,
They make the day a joyous festers.

Frogs serenade with croaky tunes,
As clouds play hopscotch 'neath the moons.
Every vine whispers gossip untrue,
While beetles boast in muddy shoe.

The empress laughs, she loves the fun,
In a world where all can run.
Her realm of green is full of play,
A whimsical land where mischief stays.

Evocative Meadows

In meadows rich with vibrant hue,
A crew of critters plans what to do.
With rabbits ready on their race,
While butterflies float with perfect grace.

The bees wear hats, it's quite the sight,
As they debate if flowers are right.
Ants march in, a conga line,
In search of snacks, oh so divine!

Snapdragons giggle at silly puns,
While clovers cheer for everyone.
In this chaos, joy finds a way,
With nature's humor on full display.

Evocative views, a playful feast,
Where laughter reigns and joy won't cease.
In the meadows, life's like a dream,
Filled with smiles, it's a joyful theme.

Garden of Fragrant Secrets

In a garden full of scents,
The daisies dance with glee,
While roses flirt with bees,
Their sweet giggles bloom, carefree.

A squirrel in a tuxedo prances,
Looking dapper, oh so spry,
He dives for acorn chances,
Underneath the bluest sky.

The herbs gossip in the breeze,
Mint swipes basil's charming hat,
Thyme whispers secrets with ease,
While oregano falls flat!

Butterflies wear fancy coats,
As ladybugs snap selfies bright,
In this garden full of quotes,
Every leaf's a delight.

Dancing with Greenery's Grace

In the forest, trees take flight,
Waltzing with the wind at night,
The roots tap to a rhythm strange,
While starlight spills, and shadows change.

A rabbit leads the funky crew,
To join the dance, a brave debut,
With hops and twirls that fill the air,
The woodland critters show they care!

Ferns shimmy, ivy swings,
Nature's band for joy it brings,
Flowers sway in vibrant hues,
Cheering for their leafy views.

The moonlight shines on every beat,
As branches sway, they find their seat,
In this green ballet of cheer,
Where laughter echoes, crystal clear.

Palettes of Natural Luxury

Painted skies with gilded hues,
Nature's brush, it boldly schmooze,
The daisies gossip, colors clash,
In extravagance, they boldly splash.

Sapphire lakes in velvet sheets,
While peacocks strut on dainty feets,
A garden party, vines entwine,
With laughter rich like vintage wine.

Sunset hues, a festive toast,
To flowers dressed in ruffled toast,
Petals giggle, silk and lace,
In this flamboyant, flowery place.

The breeze brings notes of sweet perfume,
As every bloom finds ample room,
In this lush life, let's be fancy,
Join the fun, let's dance and prance-y!

Buoyant Breezes and Blossom Dreams

With breezy whispers, dreams take flight,
As tulips twirl in sheer delight,
A wind chime's giggle fills the air,
Sweet scent swirls without a care.

Daisies toss their hats so high,
While clouds parade across the sky,
Squirrels leap with acrobatic flair,
The breeze, a jester, sends them there!

In this tomfoolery of hues,
Petals dance in playful shoes,
Bright lilacs laugh, their pranks unfurl,
In this merry, blooming world.

Bouncing laughter, fluttering cheer,
As sunbeams waltz and disappear,
Every blossom plays a role,
In this whimsical garden stroll.

Lush Canopy Dreams

Underneath the leafy crown,
I lost my shoes, and then my frown.
The squirrels giggle, birds all sway,
In this green maze, I play all day.

With fruit so ripe and sweet to bite,
I might just gain a fruity flight.
The vine's a swing, come join the fun,
In this strange jungle under the sun.

The laughter echoes, trees all shout,
A monkey steals my burger out!
In this paradise of jest and cheer,
Who knew the wild could feel so near?

As twilight calls with twinkling lights,
I dance with shadows, lose my sights.
With friends like vines, we intertwine,
In dreams of green, so sweet, divine.

Vibrant Symphony of Color

A parrot sings in hues so bright,
While I trip over my own delight.
With flowers blooming left and right,
I find my way, then lose my sight.

The bees compose a buzzing tune,
I sway along, my graceless boon.
In gardens where the daisies flirt,
I wear a hat that's full of dirt.

Each petal's brush, a painter's dream,
As I fall hard into the cream.
The colors spill, a joyful mess,
In this wild dance, I must confess.

With every bloom, my troubles fade,
A rainbow trail where laughter played.
In this vivid, zany spree,
Life's just a giggle, just like me.

Delicate Indulgence

In silky petals, dreams take flight,
A cupcake tree stands in the light.
With frosting clouds that tease my soul,
I make a wish, it's out of control.

The chocolate rain starts to pour,
As I trip on a candy floor.
With jellybeans in every hue,
I'll roll and bounce, it's fun to chew.

The sugar rush is quite the blast,
I hop along, but oh so fast!
In nibbles sweet, I find my theme,
In this delight, I'm living a dream.

A garden where the laughter grows,
And every heartbeat knows the prose.
In sugary bliss, I find my way,
Where giggles linger, come what may.

Cascading Blooms

The flowers tumble, oh what fun!
Like silly hats on everyone.
A sneaky breeze starts tickling toes,
In this wild space, where laughter flows.

The petals dance, the stalks all sway,
I join the party, hip-hip-hooray!
With butterflies as our cheerleading crew,
They flutter, giggle, and chew on dew.

A fountain sprays a shower of cheer,
I sashay right, while friends appear.
In nature's chaos, we twist and shout,
Who knew gardening could be about?

So here we play, in nature's embrace,
With blooms that spin and flowers that race.
A laughing crowd, a fragrant delight,
Cascading blooms, a gala tonight.

Gilded Geraniums

In a pot where dirt's the star,
A geranium dreams of life bizarre.
With petals bold and colors bright,
It stretches leaves in morning light.

Winking at the sun with glee,
Convincing snails to skip their spree.
It claims the porch as its domain,
While other plants just look in vain.

Chasing bees that buzz around,
It laughs at weeds, its playful sound.
With every shake, it brings delight,
Whispering secrets of the night.

A dance of blooms, a leafy show,
In gilded hues, it steals the glow.
While others wilt, it struts with flair,
A geranium, debonair.

Harvest Moon Serenade

Under the moon, the veggies grin,
Zucchini's plotting, a dizzy spin.
Tomatoes blushing, ripe and round,
In this harvest, joy abounds.

Cabbages gossip, wearing pride,
Carrots laugh as they try to hide.
A symphony of crunch and cheer,
They gather 'round for moonlit beer.

Radishes roll, what a sight to see,
Spinach twirls, wild and free.
In the garden, a quirky show,
Where produce gets its chance to glow.

With lanterns bright, they tap their toes,
As wind through leaves gives a gentle dose.
They sing of summer and fall's embrace,
In the moon's warm glow, a happy place.

Bounty of Petals

Petals dance like children free,
In springtime's breeze, a jubilee.
Daffodils wear smiles so wide,
As tulips blush with every stride.

A pollen party, bees arrive,
With buzzing tunes, they thrive alive.
Lilies sway, the stars of show,
Chasing sunbeams, to and fro.

Forget-me-nots spin tales so sweet,
Their tiny faces can't be beat.
In gardens lush, they weave delight,
Sprinkling laughter, day and night.

With fragrant laughs, they chase the gloom,
A riot of colors in every room.
These blooms declare, with petals bright,
It's fun to frolic in pure sunlight!

Eden's Secret Garden

In Eden's nook, where laughter grows,
Behind the vine, a tangle of prose.
Curly herbs in silly hats,
Tripping o'er the chubby cats.

The zucchinis plotting mischief bold,
Whispering secrets, never told.
Marigolds giggle, a cheeky crew,
With petals glimmering in morning dew.

Butterflies host a ballet grand,
Spinning wildly, a wisp of band.
A sunflower smirks, all tall and proud,
Whilst daisies wink at the nearby crowd.

In Eden's embrace, the fun unfolds,
With stories of laughter, brightly told.
Each veggie and flower plays their part,
In this quirky garden, a work of art.

Enchantment of Verdant Valleys

In a green hat that gives me glee,
I danced with frogs, they laughed at me.
The grass tickled my toes with cheer,
As crickets crooned their evening leer.

Bees buzzed by in a buzzing game,
While flowers whispered each other's name.
A squirrel wore shades, oh what a sight,
Declaring his reign, he ruled the night.

Butterflies flirted, painting the air,
They flapped their wings, without a care.
I joined a parade of ants in line,
We marched together, all looking fine.

In this valley where laughter's found,
Nature's antics truly abound.
With a wink and a smile, the world plays tricks,
Where joy and mischief merge in the mix.

Nature's Opal Embrace

In a grove where mischief grows,
I met a moose with flashy clothes.
He boasted of a glamorous life,
While juggling acorns, limiting strife.

The trees chuckled with leafy waves,
As I dodged a swarm of playful waifs.
A parrot winked, "Join in the fun!"
I tried to dance, but fell on a bun.

Clouds were cotton candy, so sweet,
While birds delivered my lunch as a treat.
I chewed on dreams and sipped on skies,
With sugar-coated wishes, oh my, oh my!

In a world where whimsy reigns supreme,
Every moment's a giddy dream.
Nature giggles, her jokes are nice,
With laughter wrapped in soft sunshine rice.

The Abundance of Moments

In a picnic where sunshine sings,
I shared my sandwich with bees and kings.
The ants lined up for a feast so grand,
As I tried to nap on a feathered strand.

This berry bush made funny faces,
With jammy smiles in all the right places.
A raccoon offered me chips and dip,
While I pretended to take a sip.

My fortune cookie said to play,
So I flipped pancakes in a silly way.
The syrup giggled all over the plate,
As if it knew we were all first-rate.

Moments stacked like fluttering leaves,
Each chuckle brings joy that never grieves.
In a world that sparkles and gleams so bright,
Every tick of the clock feels just right.

Flourishing Fantasies

In a forest where dreams take flight,
I met a rabbit dressed in white.
He sold me cookies shaped like stars,
While a hedgehog strummed on sweet guitars.

The daisies giggled as we hopped,
While dandelions danced till they dropped.
We played hide and seek with a breeze,
Spinning around as we laughed with trees.

A waterfall sang a majestic tune,
While frogs recited poems to the moon.
I sipped from a stream that flowed with glee,
And the fish winked, "Come join the spree!"

In this garden of laughter and cheer,
Every moment feels perfectly clear.
With silly dreams and fancy flight,
Our whimsical world, a pure delight!

Nature's Velvet Touch

In green gardens where shadows play,
I pluck some grass, a child's display.
Tickles and giggles, come out to stay,
As nature whispers, "Come out and play!"

Soft petals brush against my cheek,
Like little whispers, sweet and meek.
I trip on roots, oh what a streak!
With every tumble, it's joy I seek.

Bees buzzing low, in cheerful flight,
They chase the sun, from morn till night.
I join the fun, with pure delight,
In this vast world, everything feels right.

With muddy hands and sun-kissed skin,
I twirl around, let the laughter spin.
Nature's velvet touch, oh let's dive in,
In this whimsical dance, I always win!

Kaleidoscope of Fields

A patchwork quilt of colors bright,
Fields of flowers, pure delight.
I stumble through, it feels so right,
In a swirl of petals, I take flight.

Butterflies giggle as they flit,
In the sun's embrace, never sit.
I chase the blooms, I cannot quit,
In this sea of color, I'm fully lit.

Straw hats worn at a jaunty tilt,
Veggies peeking where they're built.
Confidence blooms, I strut like guilt,
In the fragrant bounty, my heart is silt.

With every step, the charm unfolds,
Nature's music, a tale retold.
I laugh and dance, in fields of gold,
A comedic day, I gladly hold.

Sipping Sunshine

With lemonade and a silly grin,
I sip my drink, let fun begin.
The ice cubes dance, they twirl and spin,
As I imagine all the crazy things I've been.

A straw that bends, a laugh that's loud,
Like bubbles burst, I'm feeling proud.
In sunlight splashes, I'm in a cloud,
A joyful heart, it draws a crowd.

Tongue-tied jokes and playful bites,
Picnic ants, oh what a sight!
Chasing shadows, chasing lights,
Chortling dreams into the night.

I raise my glass – a silly toast,
To friends who care and love the most.
In this vibrant life, I proudly boast,
With every sip, I'm the happy host.

Gentle Caress of Rain

Pitter-patter on the ground,
The raindrops dance, a silly sound.
I step outside, no care I've found,
With puddles forming all around.

Umbrella upside down, what a sight!
A soggy sock brings pure delight.
Splish-splash here, with all my might,
I leap and hop, oh what a fright!

Dripping hats and wrinkled clothes,
Laughter erupts, as nature shows.
We pirouette in rain like pros,
Our spirits lift, as everyone knows.

Dancing freely, we're all insane,
In this shower, we feel no pain.
Soaked to the bone, yet I remain,
With every laugh, I wash away the rain.

Arcadia's Dreaming Canopy

In a realm where daisies dance,
And squirrels audition for a chance,
A llama with a bow tie prances,
While bees hold buzzing romances.

The air smells sweet like jelly beans,
With mischief lurking in the greens,
A frog in shades rehearses lines,
While butterflies sip on gold wines.

Trees gossip in the breezy sun,
Chasing shadows, just for fun,
A raccoon in a top hat grins,
As laughter weaves through leafy skins.

When sunset paints the world anew,
And giggles swirl like morning dew,
In Arcadia, silly reigns supreme,
Where life's a never-ending dream.

Fronds of Untamed Joy

In jungles where the parrots sing,
A dancing sloth does his own thing,
With fruit hats perched upon his head,
He twirls about, enough said!

The monkeys play a game of tag,
Throwing coconuts, it's quite a brag,
While iguanas pull off sunbathing,
And nap on branches, just earth's lathing.

A toucan drops a fruit surprise,
The laughter echoes, fills the skies,
As vines entwine in playful flair,
Creating chaos in midair.

Underneath the laughing leaves,
The world is full of silly thieves,
Who steal the fruit but leave the fun,
In this wild world, joy's never done.

Ephemeral Hues of Opulence

In gardens painted with bright hues,
Giraffes wear shades, a funky crew,
Champagne bubbles dance with flair,
As roses giggle, debonair.

Hummingbirds buzz with snazzy moves,
In jazzy suits, they make the grooves,
While daisies tap on tiny toes,
Unruly petals for the shows.

A peacock struts in all his pride,
His feathers clash, a wild ride,
With flowers declaring, 'What a scene!'
It's opulence, but silly and keen.

As twilight hugs the vibrant view,
The night reveals its sparkly hue,
In fleeting moments, laughter swells,
In this mad garden, joy compels.

Glistening Venues at Dawn

At sunrise, roosters play the horn,
With flamingos twirling out till morn,
The critters strut in party shoes,
With eggs benedict and lively brews.

A squirrel chef flips pancakes high,
While crows serve coffee with a sigh,
And rabbits giggle, skedaddle fast,
In this venue, fun's unsurpassed.

The daisies applaud, decked in jewels,
As butterflies break all their rules,
With a toast of nectar, the dance begins,
In this dawn of laughter where joy never ends.

When the day unfurls with cheeky cheer,
And laughter fills the buoyant sphere,
In glistening venues, life's a play,
Where every moment's a bright bouquet.

www.ingramcontent.com/pod-product-compliance
Lightning Source LLC
Chambersburg PA
CBHW072220070526
44585CB00015B/1426